THE WONDER OF EASTER

Study by Lawanda Smith
Commentary by Robert Scott Nash

Free downloadable Teaching Guide for this study available at

NextSunday.com/teachingguides

NextSunday Resources
6316 Peake Road
Macon, Georgia 31210-3960
1-800-747-3016
©2016 by NextSunday Resources
All rights reserved.

TABLE OF CONTENTS

The Wonder of Easter

Study Introduction 1

Lesson 1 Proclaim Christ's Death
              1 Corinthians 11:17-32
              Study 3
              Commentary 11

Lesson 2 Remember the Resurrection
              1 Corinthians 15:1-19
              Study 19
              Commentary 27

Lesson 3 Contemplate the Mystery
              1 Corinthians 15:20-41
              Study 35
              Commentary 43

Lesson 4 Rejoice in Hope
              1 Corinthians 15:42-58
              Study 51
              Commentary 59

HOW TO USE THIS STUDY

NextSunday Resources Adult Bible Studies are designed to help adults study Scripture seriously within the context of the larger Christian tradition and, through that process, find their faith renewed, challenged, and strengthened. We study the Scriptures because we believe they affect our current lives in important ways. Each study contains the following three components:

Study Guide

Each study guide lesson is arranged in four movements:

Reflecting recalls a contemporary story, anecdote, example, or illustration to help us anticipate the session's relevance in our lives.

Studying is centered on giving the biblical material in-depth attention while often surrounding it with helpful insights from theology, ethics, church history, and other areas.

Understanding helps us find relevant connections between our lives and the biblical message.

What About Me? provides brief statements that help unite life issues with the meaning of the biblical text.

Commentary

Each study guide lesson is accompanied by an additional, in-depth commentary on the biblical material. Written by a different author than the study guide, each commentary gives the opportunity for learners to approach the Scripture text from a separate but complementary viewpoint.

Teaching Guide

In addition to the provided study guide and commentary, *NextSunday Resources* also provides a *free* downloadable teaching guide, available at NextSunday.com. Each teaching guide gives the teacher tools for focusing on the content of each study guide lesson through additional commentary and Bible background information. Through teacher helps and teaching options, each teaching guide also provides substance for variety and choice in the preparation of each lesson.

NextSunday
Resources

STUDY INTRODUCTION

In 1 Corinthians 15, Paul asserts that the message that Jesus died for our sins, was buried, and raised on the third day is "of first importance" (v. 3). It is the core of the gospel story and of the Christian faith. Therefore Easter, and Holy Week before it, point to central truths Christians would do well to remember and retell.

Rather than looking directly at Gospel accounts of Jesus' death and resurrection, this month's unit will wrestle with key texts from Paul's first letter to the Corinthians. In the Apostle's words, we will read some of the church's earliest theological reflection on the meaning of these events. First, we will explore how the church "proclaim[s] the Lord's death" (11:26) in the bread and the wine of the Lord's Supper. Then we will spend three weeks on 1 Corinthians 15, Paul's lengthy defense and interpretation of resurrection faith.

No one can claim to understand fully the meaning of Jesus' saving death and resurrection. Paul certainly made no such claim. But as much as Easter is a mystery to contemplate, it is also a hope to embrace and good news to proclaim.

Lawanda Smith teaches English and religion at Louisiana State University Alexandria. She is also pastor of a three-church charge on the weekends and does case management with Easter Seals Louisiana, working with elderly and disabled residents of central Louisiana. She enjoys reading, writing, and playing with her cats. Her newest hobby is geocaching, a worldwide game that involves "treasure hunting" with a GPS.

PROCLAIM CHRIST'S DEATH

1 Corinthians 11:17-32

Central Question

What place does the Lord's Supper have in my spiritual journey?

Scripture

1 Corinthians 11:17-32 17 Now in the following instructions I do not commend you, because when you come together it is not for the better but for the worse. 18 For, to begin with, when you come together as a church, I hear that there are divisions among you; and to some extent I believe it. 19 Indeed, there have to be factions among you, for only so will it become clear who among you are genuine. 20 When you come together, it is not really to eat the Lord's supper. 21 For when the time comes to eat, each of you goes ahead with your own supper, and one goes hungry and another becomes drunk. 22 What! Do you not have homes to eat and drink in? Or do you show contempt for the church of God and humiliate those who have nothing? What should I say to you? Should I commend you? In this matter I do not commend you! 23 For I received from the Lord what I also handed on to you, that the Lord Jesus on the night when he was betrayed took a loaf of bread, 24 and when he had given thanks, he broke it and said, "This is my body that is for you. Do this in remembrance of me." 25 In the same way he took the cup also, after supper, saying, "This cup is the new covenant in my blood. Do this, as often as you drink it, in remembrance of me." 26 For as often as you eat this bread and drink the cup, you proclaim the Lord's death until he comes. 27 Whoever, therefore, eats the bread or drinks the cup of the Lord in an unworthy manner will be answerable for the body and blood of the Lord. 28 Examine yourselves, and only then eat of the bread and drink of the cup. 29 For all who eat and drink without discerning the body, eat and drink judgment against themselves. 30 For this reason many of you are weak and ill, and some have died. 31 But if we judged ourselves, we would not be judged. 32 But when we are judged by the Lord, we are disciplined so that we may not be condemned along with the world.

Reflecting

One of my best friends and her family now live eight hours and three states away from me. Prior to their move three years ago, they lived about twelve miles from my house. Over the six years that we were close by, Melanie and I became fast friends. We talked almost every day, and we enjoyed simple things like running errands together.

One of the habits we developed—and one we enjoyed the most—was eating together once a week. Sometimes we would go out to grab a bite, and other times we would get together at her house or at mine, and the host would cook a meal. We enjoyed trying new recipes, but the most meaningful part of our gatherings was the conversation and the laughter that went along with those meals.

Eventually, my friend's husband was transferred to another city, and soon the family moved. I still remember the last evening we got together at their house for a meal. The conversation wasn't as lighthearted as usual because we knew it would be our last meal together for a while. We didn't quite know how to say goodbye. We've stayed in close contact since Melanie moved, and we still share recipes over e-mail. Every time I try one of those recipes, I'm reminded of the meals we shared together in the past, especially that last meal we enjoyed at her house in Louisiana.

Sharing a meal is an intimate experience. Usually close friends or family

> **?** What memories do you cherish of meals shared with loved ones? What made those meals special?

members dine together, and mealtime is often the occasion for good conversation. In ancient Jewish culture, sharing a meal was a symbol of hospitality. Nowhere is that more evident than in the last supper Jesus shared with his disciples.

Studying

Palm Sunday commemorates the day when Jesus rode into Jerusalem on a borrowed donkey with crowds of men, women, and children waving palm branches, throwing their cloaks on the ground in front of him, and shouting nationalistic slogans. They had all heard the rumor that Jesus was the political savior who would deliver them from their enemies.

Usually on this Sunday of remembrance, we focus on the Scripture passage containing the triumphal procession into Jerusalem. But Thursday of this week, the day before Good Friday, is another high point in Holy Week. In some traditions, it is known as Maundy Thursday. The word "Maundy" is derived from the word "mandate," coming from Jesus' mandate that disciples love each other as he has loved them (Jn 13:34-35).

Maundy Thursday is also the day we celebrate Jesus' last meal with his disciples, which he shared with them before his arrest and crucifixion. He washed their feet and shared with them the loaf of bread and the cup of wine. This tradition is the focus of today's session.

The context of our Scripture passage is the early church at Corinth. If there was ever a church that had divisions and difficulties, the Corinthian church was it. That conflict was evident even when they shared the Lord's Supper together.

Apparently, the people of the Corinthian church had turned their experience of the Lord's Supper into quite a party. The observance of that supper came in the context of another meal, one in which the rich had more than enough food and drink—even eating and drinking in excess—while the poor, probably slaves and servants, arrived and departed hungry. No one, it seemed, remembered what sharing the Lord's Supper was all about.

So the Apostle Paul reminded them. The supper was not to be a party but a memorial of Christ's death. Before partaking of this supper, worshipers needed to take stock of their own lives.

It's not insignificant that in some Christian traditions, the Lord's Supper is known as "Communion." Paul reminded the Christians at Corinth that the Supper was a symbol of their communion with Christ and with each other.

Certainly the Supper is a memorial of Jesus' death. But when we say it is *only* a memorial, we diminish its significance. According to Paul, when Christians remembered Jesus' death, they also remembered his life of sacrificial giving, which culminated in his ultimate sacrifice when he gave his life on the cross. That sacrificial giving was the direct opposite of what the Corinthian Christians were doing. In their way of "celebrating" the Lord's Supper, the insiders were starkly separated from those considered the outsiders. Instead of giving sacrificially in order to include those who had the least, the rich simply celebrated excessively while the poor were left out.

> The cup of blessing that we bless, is it not a sharing in the blood of Christ? The bread that we break, is it not a sharing in the body of Christ? Because there is one bread, we who are many are one body, for we all partake of the one bread. (1 Cor 10:16-17)

Paul admonished the Corinthian Christians that if they were hungry, they should eat before they left home so that their focus could be on the memorial of Jesus' death when they came together. The memory of Jesus' sacrifice should encourage their sacrificial giving in response.

When Paul reminds his readers that the bread is the body of Christ, he doesn't add the familiar phrase "broken for you." Jesus' body was broken for others, but apparently Paul did not want to focus on brokenness. Perhaps the church at Corinth was already broken enough. Paul wanted the observance of the Lord's Supper and the memory of Jesus' sacrifice to bring the church together, not break it apart.

When they remembered Jesus' sacrificial life and his ultimate sacrifice of death, the Corinthian Christians were to respond with love for Christ and for each other rather than with divisiveness. They were to be drawn together in nothing less than Holy

Communion. They were to be the body of Christ, united under his sacrifice to serve each other.

Understanding

When my mother knew she was dying, she called her family together one day and told us that she knew we would remember the trying times and her final struggles with life. There is no way we could forget those days. But Mom said when we remembered her, she also wanted us to remember the good times we spent with her. To be sure, what I remember most about my mother was that she always gave unselfishly of herself to her family, her students, and her friends. She always looked for the best in everyone, even those people others might want to dismiss.

With his sharing of the Last Supper, Jesus wanted his disciples—both then and now—to remember his death, his ultimate sacrifice even for his enemies. He also wanted them to remember every other part of his sacrificial life and to look forward to his resurrection and his coming again.

Paul admonished the Corinthian Christians to take stock of their lives and ask forgiveness for their sin before observing the Lord's Supper, and we should do the same. In many Christian traditions, there is a time set aside for corporate confession of sin and recognition of Christ's forgiveness of sin even while we were yet sinners. If we take such confession seriously and do not treat it as only a recital of words, it can be very significant.

Other Christians prefer to take stock of their lives silently before partaking of the Lord's Supper. However we choose to do so, taking an inward look at our hearts and examining our intentions toward others is an essential prerequisite to our accepting the bread and the cup. Sometimes, even though we may not be as divided as the Corinthian Christians, we still can overlook the importance of confession, repentance, and the acceptance of forgiveness. Sometimes observing the Lord's Supper is just another ritual of the church. But when we take time to remember the significance, it becomes a way of refocusing our lives.

The main character in Alice Walker's short story "The Welcome Table" is an elderly African American woman who walks into an all-white church one Sunday morning. At first, the congregation just looks at her, not sure what to do. Eventually, some people ask her if she knows where she is, and others even suggest that she might need to leave. But the woman stays there, sitting quietly on the back row, until finally someone escorts her out. Then, the woman simply walks down the path, singing the words of an old spiritual, "One day I'm going to feast at the Welcome Table." That's what the Lord's Supper table is to be for Christians, a welcome table where all are included and no one is made to feel less than anyone else.

The temptation at this time of year is to rush into Easter. At least a month—or maybe two months—before Easter Sunday, we see reminders all over the secular world. Department stores reduce prices on Easter finery, knowing that virtually every child will want a new outfit for Easter. Then comes the display of Easter candy, brightly dyed Easter eggs, yellow chicks, and fluffy white bunny rabbits.

In the *Didache* (first century), the prayer over the bread reflects on the church as scattered and "broken" at present, but one day gathered together into the kingdom of God:

We give you thanks, our Father, for the life and knowledge you made known to us through Jesus your Servant. To you be glory for ever. As this broken bread was scattered upon the mountains, but was brought together and became one, so let your church be gathered together from the ends of the earth into your kingdom, for yours is the glory and the power through Jesus Christ for ever. (*Didache* 9:3-4)

There's nothing intrinsically wrong with any of these things. Butterflies, bunnies, chicks, eggs, and most all the symbols of Easter are actually symbols of the new life we celebrate in the resurrection. However, the commercial emphasis tempts us to rush to Easter without first going to the cross.

As any mother will profess, pain comes before bringing new life into the world. When we go through the darkness and the pain before getting to new life, we appreciate that new life even more.

Beginning with Palm Sunday and proceeding to Maundy Thursday, Good Friday, and Holy Saturday, this Holy Week will be a week of darkness. It's not an easy week. If we take seriously

the remembrance of Jesus' journey to the cross, his crucifixion and his death, this week will be dark and hard. Truthfully, sometimes we don't want to go there.

But as the mystic John of the Cross reflected, the dark night of the soul is when Christ may reach out to us the most, for when we are hurting, we may be most open to God's compassion.

Yet as dark as it is, this week need not be a week of despair. As an old saying also reminds us, the darkest hour is just before dawn. We can't fully experience the exuberance of Resurrection Sunday unless we go through these darkest days. Yet, though Thursday, Friday, and Saturday are coming, we hold on to the thought that Sunday is also coming.

What About Me?

• *We must take stock of our lives.* At what points might we have been selfish, thinking more of ourselves than of others? What unconfessed sin might we have in our lives? The saying may be old, but it is still true: confession is good for the soul.

• *We must think of others who need to be included.* It's easy to associate primarily with people who are like us. But we also need to ask, "Who are the 'least of these' around us?" With whom do we need to share what we have?

• *We must work to heal divisions in our church.* Sometimes church members divide over petty problems and sometimes over significant events and decisions in the life of the congregation. This season, what can we do to identify and move toward healing these divisions? How can we begin redemptive conversations with each other?

Resources

Raymond Brown, "1 Corinthians," *The Broadman Bible Commentary*, vol. 10 (Nashville: Broadman, 1970).

Alice Walker, "The Welcome Table," *Listening for God*, ed. Paula J. Carlson and Peter S. Hawkins (Minneapolis: Augsburg Fortress, 1994).

PROCLAIM
CHRIST'S DEATH

1 Corinthians 11:17-32

Introduction

The old saying, "One picture is worth a thousand words," could not be truer of the Lord's Supper. The Apostle Paul wrote that when we eat the bread and drink the cup of the Lord's Supper we are proclaiming Christ's death until he comes (11:26). Without words but with quiet, reverent partaking of the elements of this simple meal, we are giving testimony to our faith that God has worked graciously in the death of Christ to bind us together as one in God's love.

After she retired from nursing, my grandmother went to art school and began to paint landscapes and portraits. She used to tell me that the frame "makes or breaks" the picture. So it is with the beautiful picture we have in the Lord's Supper. The frame for that picture is the church. The message of the supper is complimented or distorted by the quality of unity that exists within the body of Christ. A healthy, harmonious church frames the picture well. A sick, contentious church obscures the picture so that its message cannot be conveyed.

Paul's instruction to the church at Corinth about the Lord's Supper appears in a long section of the letter in which he addresses several problems that arose whenever the church was gathered for worship (1 Cor 11:2–14:40). We should keep in mind, therefore, that his words regarding Communion are framed in the context of problem-solving. Paul was not trying to outline his theology of the Lord's Supper; he was trying to correct a Corinthian practice that dishonored the meal and its message.

The section can be divided into three parts. First, Paul identifies the problem in the Corinthians' practice (vv. 17-22). Next, he reminds them of the tradition he has passed on to them (vv. 23-26). In the third part, verses 27-32 (and actually extending to v. 34), he discusses the consequences of their improper practice.

I. Barriers to Proclaiming the Lord's Death (vv. 17-22)

The Lord's Supper proclaims the oneness of Christ's body. Though his body was broken and his blood was spilled, his death has united us to him and each other by the saving grace of God. Although many churches observe the Lord's Supper today by serving individual portions of bread and drink, the early church appears to have used a single loaf of bread and a common cup. The significance of the oneness of the body of Christ represented by the single loaf and cup can sometimes be lost when we pass around "a pan full of cracker crumbs and thimbles full of grape juice," as the late New Testament scholar Frank Stagg used to describe it. The greatest threat to the message of oneness the Lord's Supper proclaims, however, comes when the body of Christ is divided.

In these verses, Paul informs the Corinthian Christians that he has heard divisions exist within their fellowship. He also addressed the problem of divisions earlier in the letter (1:10–4:21). Those divisions involved different groups lining up behind different leaders. The divisions in chapter 11 involve differences between richer and poorer church members. To understand why such divisions arose, we need to recognize two important features of their observance of the Lord's Supper.

First of all, we need to remember *where* they assembled. No church buildings yet existed, and most public buildings were not suitable for such a meeting. They could meet in the open air, but the harsh summer sun and the frequent, cold rains of winter often made it difficult to do so. In Corinth, as elsewhere, the early Christians regularly met in the homes of members. But which members? Most members did not own their own homes, and very few would have had homes large enough to contain the whole church, or even a significant part of it. Paul confirms in verse 26 that not many of the church members were wise, powerful, or of noble birth. Only a few of them, then, would have owned homes big enough for the church to assemble and observe the Lord's Supper. In his letter to the Romans, which Paul wrote while in Corinth, he identifies a man named Gaius as "host for the whole church" (16:23). In 1 Corinthians 16:19, writing to Corinth from Ephesus, Paul sends greetings from the former Corinthian ministers Aquila and Prisca and "the church *in their house*." The early Christians were dependent on the hospitality of wealthier members to provide space in which to assemble.

Secondly, the Lord's Supper was not simply observed as a ritual in the context of a church worship service. It was part of a larger meal. In later centuries, the church sometimes distinguished between a meal called the agape feast and the Lord's Supper, but in the early days the Lord's Supper was not separated from the fellowship dinner. Dinners took place in most large homes in a room called the *triclinium*, so called because people reclined along three sides of the room. The maximum number of reclining diners in most homes was nine. If the person hosting the church followed the normal pattern, then eight people would have reclined with the host in the *triclinium* while the rest gathered in the only other available space in the home, the atrium or courtyard. One suspects that the people invited to dine in the *triclinium* would have been similar in status and wealth to the host. Thus, the division between rich and poor would have been obvious every time the church gathered to observe the meal.

Paul seems to reflect on this rich-poor division in his criticism of their practice: "For when the time comes to eat, each of you goes ahead with his own supper, and one goes hungry and another becomes drunk" (v. 21). They appear to have been divided not only by the walls of the house but also by the amount of food apportioned. Some gorged themselves; some barely got leftovers. One can imagine that those whom Paul criticized for "going ahead with his own supper" were the wealthier members refusing to wait for the poorer members who probably had to work longer hours before arriving. Their indulgence in their affluence mocked the message of the one table of the one Lord. They humiliated the have-nots, and Paul condemned such a practice (v. 22).

II. A Reminder of What Is Proclaimed (vv. 23-26)

The word "tradition" refers to a teaching, practice, or custom that is handed down from one person or group to another. The purpose of tradition is to keep alive an important belief or action. It also serves to unite later generations to those that began the tradition. Some traditions eventually fall by the wayside because they no longer speak meaningfully to later generations. Sometimes letting go of a tradition is necessary in order to follow the Spirit's lead into new vistas of awareness and service. Sometimes, however, the demise of a tradition means the loss of something vital to the faith and a loss of connection with the larger family of faith through the ages.

In 1 Corinthians 11:23-26, Paul calls the Corinthians' attention back to the tradition he had received from the Lord and "handed over" to them. Paul reminds them that on the night when Jesus was "handed over," he gave them bread to eat and said, "Do this in remembrance of *me*." Likewise, he gave them the cup to drink "in remembrance of *me*." In doing this, Paul writes, "you proclaim the Lord's *death* until he comes" (11:26). Paul's words stress that the Lord's Supper is to be focused on the Lord, not on filling the belly. The gospel of the crucified Lord who gave himself for us is the message of the meal. To treat the dinner as one of self-indulgence, especially without regard for the have-nots, means that it is no longer the Lord's Supper (v. 20).

Paul's words that recall the last supper Jesus observed with his disciples in the upper room comprise the earliest account we have of that event. Paul carefully chose his language. Christ was "handed over" for us: "This is my body which is *for you*" (v. 24). Paul received the tradition about the last supper from the Lord and "handed it over" to the Corinthians. The mysterious, miraculous event of the cross occurred for the sake of God's people. The glorious tradition of the Lord's Supper was also given to God's people as a powerful testimony of what transpired in the cross. In participating in this meal, the church shares in the ongoing proclamation of the message of the cross. They do it not simply looking back to that one determining moment when Christ died, however. They do it looking forward in faithful anticipation of that crowning moment when Christ's victory is complete.

III. Consequences of Distorting the Proclamation (vv. 27-32)

Some traditions are so central to the Christian faith that to lose, neglect, or distort them is catastrophic to the integrity of faith itself. To neglect or distort the tradition of the Lord's Supper is to lose contact with the central message of the gospel that through Christ's death we have been united to each other and to God.

The last three words of verse 26, "until he comes," flow into the third part where Paul speaks about judgment. Elsewhere in the letter, Paul refers to the judgment that will occur when the Lord returns (1:7-8; 3:8, 13-15; 4:5; 5:5). The Lord's Supper is a testimony that the one whose body was broken and whose blood was spilled shall return in triumph and judge the world.

Exactly what Paul meant by "not discerning the Lord's body" in verse 29 is unclear. Some see it referring to the actual body of Christ. Not to "discern" it would be not to recognize the significance of his death. Some see it referring to the elements of the supper. If one fails to see that the bread and wine are the body and blood of Christ, then one physically ingests spiritual judgment. Others think it refers to the church as Christ's body. If one fails to appreciate the value of the people who make up the church, then one brings judgment on oneself. It is likely that Paul means both Christ's physical body given on the cross and the church as his continuing body. For Paul, the two are joined together. Christ's suffering was for the sake of the church. Those who indulge in his supper without regard for his broken, bleeding body or for that body of the redeemed for which he died are guilty of profaning his body (v. 27). Eating and drinking "without discerning the body" means missing the message that Christ really died for all of us. That is, we are united into the body of Christ through his death. If we dishonor a part of his body—as the rich Corinthians were dishonoring the poor—we dishonor the meaning of his death and bring judgment on ourselves.

Paul considers this such a serious offense that he asserts that some have become ill or died because they dishonored Christ's body (v. 30). For some, these words suggest that Paul saw the

Lord's Supper as magical. If one misused the magic, there could be harmful effects. Others suggest that Paul had in mind the properties of medicine as they were understood in antiquity. People knew then, as we know now, that medicine can become deadly if abused. We may reject both of these notions, but we should keep in mind that Paul did not radically separate the spiritual from the physical. In 1 Corinthians 6:12-20 he went to great lengths to argue that what one does with the body affects one's spiritual self. The reverse is also true. What one does spiritually has an impact on one's physical self. Paul indicates that judgment inflicted on the church by the Lord is for disciplinary purposes rather than condemnation (11:32). Thus, the church as a whole should take the illness and death of some as warning signs.

Better still, Paul urges, Christians should take pains to judge themselves (v. 31). We usually understand his admonition to "examine ourselves" in verse 28 to be a call for individual soul-searching. It may be that, but it is also more. The church as a whole is called to examine itself, to judge itself, to correct itself whenever it has distorted the proclamation of Christ's death through divisiveness or discrimination. Christ died for *all*. So, individually and collectively, we should examine and judge ourselves to see if our practice actually proclaims the Lord's death. How will Christ judge us "when he comes"?

Notes

Notes

2

REMEMBER THE RESURRECTION

1 Corinthians 15:1-19

Central Question

What difference does the resurrection of Christ make?

Scripture

1 Corinthians 15:1-19 1 Now I would remind you, brothers and sisters, of the good news that I proclaimed to you, which you in turn received, in which also you stand, 2 through which also you are being saved, if you hold firmly to the message that I proclaimed to you—unless you have come to believe in vain. 3 For I handed on to you as of first importance what I in turn had received: that Christ died for our sins in accordance with the scriptures, 4 and that he was buried, and that he was raised on the third day in accordance with the scriptures, 5 and that he appeared to Cephas, then to the twelve. 6 Then he appeared to more than five hundred brothers and sisters at one time, most of whom are still alive, though some have died. 7 Then he appeared to James, then to all the apostles. 8 Last of all, as to one untimely born, he appeared also to me. 9 For I am the least of the apostles, unfit to be called an apostle, because I persecuted the church of God. 10 But by the grace of God I am what I am, and his grace toward me has not been in vain. On the contrary, I worked harder than any of them—though it was not I, but the grace of God that is with me. 11 Whether then it was I or they, so we proclaim and so you have come to believe. 12 Now if Christ is proclaimed as raised from the dead, how can some of you say there is no resurrection of the dead? 13 If there is no resurrection of the dead, then Christ has not been raised; 14 and if Christ has not been raised, then our proclamation has been in vain and your faith has been in vain. 15 We are even found to be misrepresenting God, because we testified of God that he raised Christ—whom he did not raise if it is true that the dead are not raised. 16 For if the dead are not raised, then Christ has not been raised. 17 If Christ has not been raised, your faith is futile and you are still in your sins. 18 Then those also who have died in Christ have perished. 19 If for this life only we have hoped in Christ, we are of all people most to be pitied.

Reflecting

It was one of those times I'll never forget, one of those times when everything fell into place. I had just returned from skiing in Colorado, and with a few days left of semester break I had settled in at my parents' house in north Louisiana about three miles south of the Arkansas state line. The weather forecast called for a few inches of snow, and I could hardly wait.

I love snow, and even though I had spent the last several days playing in lots of snow, I looked forward to more. The prospect of even one or two inches excited me. But by mid-afternoon, when no snow had arrived, I lay down for my ritual Sunday afternoon nap.

My dad awakened me early that evening. "You'd better go outside soon," he said, "or you'll miss the four flakes of snow!" I hopped up. Those few flakes could mean only one thing, I thought. More snow was on the way. Donning hiking boots and a thick sweater, I headed outside.

An hour later, I was back inside, exchanging my hiking boots and sweater for snow boots and ski clothes that I hadn't even unpacked yet. Those two predicted inches of snow had turned into four and then five. By morning, a fresh eight-inch blanket of snow covered the ground.

After traipsing through the snow for most of the morning, I went in for a cup of hot chocolate. Suddenly, something hit the sliding glass door. Dashing out to the patio, I discovered a small bird, seemingly lifeless on the concrete. Desperate to save its life,

I cuddled it in my hands, rubbing it gently and trying to keep it warm. To my amazement, that bird began to move. Eventually, its eyes opened. Finally, when it warmed up enough and got its bearings, the tiny, revived bird fluttered off toward the woods. It was a small symbol of resurrection, there in the deepest, coldest part of winter.

Resurrection Sunday is the day when we remember Christ's resurrection and celebrate new life for today.

Studying

Not only was the church at Corinth arguing over practices surrounding the proper observance of the Lord's Supper (11:17-34), but they also were having theological disputes. In particular, the Apostle Paul addresses the fact that some people in that congregation did not believe in the possibility of resurrection. There is no indication that the Corinthians had specifically asked Paul to advise them on this issue. He doesn't preface his remarks with "now concerning" as he does with matters that seem to have been raised in a prior letter the Corinthians sent to him (7:1, 25; 8:1; 12:1). Most likely, Paul learned about the theological controversy orally from those who had delivered the Corinthian letter (1:11; 16:17).

Paul's argument is logical. He first lists distinctive Christian beliefs that could serve as a confession of faith. Paul takes the Corinthian believers back to the basics, "to the very foundation of their faith" (Soards, 1185-86). His first point is that the common tradition of the church has always included belief in the resurrection. In verses 3-8 we find a creed-like statement of the content of the Christian faith. Except for Paul's comments in verse 6b ("most of whom are still alive," etc.) and verse 8 ("last of all...he appeared to me"), this section should be understood as pre-Pauline tradition that formed the basis of Paul's preaching from the beginning of his ministry in Corinth. The Apostle introduces the section with the language of "receiving" and "handing on": the customary rabbinic terminology for passing on an oral tradition from teacher to student.

What was this tradition? Christ died for our sins in accordance with the Scriptures. He was buried, and he was raised on the third day in accordance with the Scriptures. He appeared to Cephas and then to the twelve. Then he appeared to more than 500 brothers and sisters at the same time. Next, he appeared to James and others. The essence of the Christian faith is found in the story of Jesus' saving work, organized around four important verbs: "Christ *died*, he was *buried*, he was *raised*, and he *appeared*" to the disciples (Talbert, 122).

The final verb, "appeared," is used or implied six times in verses 5-8, culminating in Paul's assertion that Jesus appeared to him "last of all." Unlike the others, Paul was not privy to any post-resurrection appearances in the days immediately after the crucifixion. His encounter on the Damascus Road came months if not years later. Therefore, Paul qualifies his experience by describing himself as "one untimely born." This unusual Greek word (*ektroma*) could be interpreted in two ways. It might mean "born too late," that is, long after the others to whom Christ appeared. More likely, the implication is "born prematurely," setting Paul's rapid, dramatic conversion in contrast to the months or years of spiritual "gestation" the other eyewitnesses to the resurrection experienced before their encounter with the risen Christ. In either case, Paul is subtly admitting that his experience of the risen Christ did not fit the expected pattern. It was mistimed, although no less significant.

Paul's second point is found in verse 6, where he mentions that some eyewitnesses were still alive, although some had died. Even for those who have experienced the risen Christ, death has not yet been destroyed. This means that the resurrection of believers is still to be anticipated in the future (Talbert, 122).

In verses 12-19, Paul challenges an assertion made by the troublesome faction among the Corinthians: "How can some of you say there is no resurrection of the dead?" This faction obviously believed in Christ's resurrection. The problem was that they believed they had already been raised with him (1 Cor 4:8; see 2 Tim 2:17-18). It seems that they denied a future resurrection such as Paul affirms in verse 19.

Paul responds to this assertion by laying out the consequences that follow from what the Corinthians are saying. If there is no (future) resurrection, then Christ has not been raised, Paul's preaching is in vain, their faith is in vain, they are still in their sins, and those who have died in the faith have utterly perished.

If Christ has not been raised, Paul declares, then his proclamation and the proclamation of other Christians has been a monumental waste of time. In fact, the many eyewitnesses he noted earlier were all misrepresenting God. If Christ has not been raised, faith is ultimately futile. And if we have hope in this life only, we are to be pitied.

Paul's argument rests on the fact that Christ is indeed risen from the dead. Not only that, but as a result believers are no longer dead in their sins but are instead alive in Christ. It is for this reason that we celebrate Resurrection Sunday.

> This whole section resists viewing Christ's resurrection in isolation as a mythic theme or as an eternal timeless truth. Paul's argument exposes the errors of the Corinthians' denial of a future resurrection of the dead. Paul argues a tight logical loop: *Christ is raised* > the gospel is preached > the Corinthians have faith > the dead in Christ are raised > *Christ is raised*. To falsify one element of this loop is to invalidate the whole, and to invalidate the loop exposes the testimony of the apostles as false testimony about God. If, moreover, the testimony about God's gracious saving work is false, then, the dead are lost and Christians have no hope, but are to be pitied as deluded. (Soards, 1187)

Understanding

What does believing in the resurrection mean for us today? Admittedly, people hold different theological positions about the nature of the resurrection, but belief in Christ's resurrection is still central to the Christian faith.

In her short story "A Good Man Is Hard to Find," Flannery O'Connor's main character, The Misfit, declares that Jesus is the only person who ever raised anyone from the dead. The Misfit continues to say that if Jesus did what he claimed to do, there's nothing for us to do but to drop everything and follow him.

Ironically, The Misfit is the only one in the story who gets this point.

It's a significant point. Remembering the resurrection should begin with the memory of the stone rolled away from an empty tomb on that first Easter morning. That event is a foundation of our Christian beliefs. But remembering Christ's resurrection also has implications for today. Paul might go so far as to say that if the resurrection doesn't make a difference, our faith is in vain. In Paul's view, if Christ is risen, then we as followers of Christ are risen in Christ (see Phil 3). In fact, Paul says we are dead to our old life and risen as new creatures.

Most often, this new creature is interpreted individually. Individual persons are born again as new creations. The fruits of the spirit include love, joy, peace, longsuffering, and faithfulness. Each person is a new creature who exhibits these fruits. But New Testament scholar Marcus Borg reminds us that there is also a communal element to this new creation (110). Our new "communal identity" subverts the sharpest of boundaries. Indeed, Paul said to the Galatians, "In Christ there is neither Greek nor Jew, male nor female, slave nor free" (Gal 3:28). All are equal in Christ.

This admonition is just as relevant for us today as it was for the divided Christians in Corinth. Sometimes we find ourselves arguing over the details of our faith, whether they involve belief or practice. The implication of Paul's words is that if we are risen with Christ, such

> Note how the theological underpinnings of 1 Corinthians have evolved: the wisdom of God revealed in the cross (1 Cor 1:18ff.) culminates in the mystery of God revealed through resurrection. Between cross and resurrection lie the responsibilities of the community of faith. (Wilson, 173)

disagreements should not be so sharp that they divide Christians. There is room for diversity in the details, to be sure, but we must strive for unity in what is central to our faith.

What About Me?

• *Easter should make a difference in our everyday lives.* The resurrection is not something we remember and celebrate only once a year. What does it mean for us today that Christ is risen? What difference does it make in the way we lead our lives?

• *Believing in the resurrection means we are resurrected with Christ.* The New Testament generally, and Paul in particular, links the resurrection of Christ with the resurrection of believers. This is not only a hope for the future but a transforming reality in the present. We are new creatures with Christ-like spirits of passion and compassion.

• *Resurrection Sunday is a significant event in our faith journey.* Because Christ is alive, we are alive and should enjoy life. The Easter season celebrates the many ways Christ's triumph over death renews and transforms our spiritual lives.

References

Marcus Borg, *The Heart of Christianity* (San Francisco: HarperSanFrancisco, 2003).

Raymond B. Brown, "I Corinthians," *The Broadman Bible Commentary*, vol. 10 (Nashville: Broadman, 1970).

Flannery O'Connor, "A Good Man Is Hard to Find," *Flannery O'Connor: Collected Works* (New York: Library of America, 1988).

Marion L. Soards, "1 Corinthians," *Mercer Commentary on the Bible*, ed. Watson E. Mills et al. (Macon GA: Mercer University Press, 1995).

Charles H. Talbert, *Reading Corinthians*, rev. ed. (Macon GA: Smyth & Helwys, 2002).

Richard F. Wilson, "Corinthian Correspondence," *Mercer Dictionary of the Bible*, ed. Watson E. Mills et al. (Macon GA: Mercer University Press, 1990).

REMEMBER THE RESURRECTION

1 Corinthians 15:1-19

Introduction

I once preached a sermon on the Sunday following Easter titled "Vampires, Ghosts, and Zombies." When I told my wife, Dawn, the title of my sermon, she responded, "I thought we were in the season of Easter, not Halloween." I asked her, "What do vampires, ghosts, and zombies all have in common?" She replied, "They're all dead." "No," I answered, "they don't stay dead." "Oh, just like Jesus," she said. "Yes, just like Jesus."

Like the characters of innumerable horror movies, Jesus did not stay dead. Like those characters, too, when Jesus came back from the dead, he came back different. He was transformed into a different kind of existence. Unlike those movie monsters, however, the transformed Jesus did not come back to wreak havoc or terrify people. Jesus came back to save people. In fact, his resurrection is an essential part of God's redemption of the whole creation. His resurrection gives us the basis for hope in our own transformation into new creatures and for hope in our own resurrection.

The resurrection of Jesus was a historical event. For some people, both inside and outside the church, accepting the historical reality of Jesus' resurrection is as difficult as believing in vampires, ghosts, and zombies. According to Acts 17:32, when Paul preached about the resurrection of the dead in Athens, some of the listeners mocked him. Some of the believers in Corinth apparently also had doubts about the resurrection. They do not appear to have doubted that Jesus had been raised from the dead. What some of them seem to have found incredible was that Jesus' *body* had been raised. They could accept that Jesus' spirit or soul had survived death and that theirs would, too (somewhat like ghosts). The idea that bodies of flesh could be raised, though, sounded too much like tales of vampires and zombies.

I. The Message of First Importance (vv. 1-11)

After dealing with a variety of behavioral problems that plagued the young church in Corinth in chapters 1–14, Paul turns to address a major matter of belief. Confusion regarding this matter may well have caused some of the behavioral problems, so, in a sense, Paul is now getting to the root of the matter. He reminds them of the gospel he preached to them. They received this gospel and have taken their stand on it. Through it they are being saved—if they hold fast to it.

Then Paul recites for them a part of the gospel that he calls "of first importance." The recitation appears to be an early creedal statement that had been passed on to Paul, who passed it on to them. It states,

> Christ died for our sins in accordance with the Scriptures;
> he was buried;
> he was raised on the third day in accordance with Scriptures;
> he appeared to Cephas, then to the twelve.

The statement affirms that Christ's death and resurrection were "in accordance with Scriptures," that is, the Old Testament. The early church inherited its Scriptures from Judaism but interpreted them in the light of Jesus Christ. Passages of the Bible that originally spoke about other matters were reinterpreted to apply to Jesus. For example, Jesus was seen as the fulfillment of the passage in Isaiah 53 about the suffering of God's servant for our sins. Psalms that praise God for delivering the righteous from death (such as Ps 16) were viewed as references to Jesus' resurrection. The statement, "he was buried," confirms that Jesus really did die, while the appearances to Cephas and the twelve serve to confirm that he really was raised from the dead. The importance of the witnesses to Christ's resurrection leads Paul to add to the creedal statement other sources that confirm the events. Jesus appeared to more than 500 believers at one time, Paul asserts, stressing that most of them are still alive—in case anyone needs to check out their story. He then appeared to James, the leader of the Jerusalem church, and to all the apostles.

To this impressive list of witnesses Paul adds his own name. When Paul refers to himself here as "one untimely born," he uses a word that often referred to an abortion, a miscarriage, or a deformed newborn. It has here the sense of one who is "born prematurely." We might think in terms of a caesarean birth. Paul did not come to his new life in Christ in an expected way; he was taken by God from the womb of his old life and suddenly "birthed" as a new Paul when he met the resurrected Christ. This fits well with the accounts of his conversion found in the book of Acts. Paul insists that he was undeserving of this new birth and unfit to be numbered among the apostles because of his earlier persecution of the church. By the grace of God, however, he was reborn as an apostle. God's gift of new life to Paul was not wasted, either. Though he might be the least of the apostles, Paul emphasizes that he worked harder than the rest. As this sounds a bit boastful, Paul explains that it was actually the grace of God working through him.

Paul then reinforces why he has reminded them of the message "of first importance" and why he has supported it with his list of witnesses. All of us preached the same message about the resurrected Christ, he insists, and you yourselves believed it. Verse 11 takes us back to verses 1-2. This is the message the Corinthians received, the one they have taken their stand on, and the one that is saving them—unless they have believed this message "in vain" (v. 2).

The word translated "in vain" can be taken two ways. (1) Perhaps the testimony is unreliable. Perhaps the witnesses were wrong. Perhaps Christ was not raised. If so, then they have been deceived and their faith is pointless. (2) An alternative way to translate the last part of verse 2 is "unless you believed *incoherently.*" In other words, they have heard the message of first importance, but they do not really "get it." They have not seen the full implications of what it means to believe that Christ has been raised from the dead. What follows supports both of these ways of understanding what Paul means. Paul considers the implications if Christ were not raised. He also gives attention to the misunderstanding some of the Corinthians have about the nature and meaning of Christ's resurrection.

When I was doing doctoral work, I once had to present a colloquium paper on a new book on Paul written by a famous scholar. In my research, I discovered that the new book reflected a phenomenal change in perspective from the author's earlier writings. He had previously belonged to the school of thought that saw the resurrection of Jesus as a mythological story. In order to find the core of the Christian message, he believed one had to remove the fantastic elements and realize that the resurrection simply enables us to see ourselves differently. In the new book, however, the author argued that the historical reality of the resurrection was the core of the gospel. To eliminate the resurrection as a real event was to remove the basis for believing in God's ultimate triumph over evil. It also rendered meaningless not only Christ's suffering and death but also our own lives and our own suffering. In short, he had come to see that the resurrection of Christ is a matter "of first importance."

II. The Consequences of Denying the Message (vv. 12-19)

The story mentioned above involves more than biblical scholarship. I learned that this person's change in perspective about Christ's resurrection had emerged from personal experience as well as professorial reflection. Alcoholism and the threat of losing his job brought him to a crisis. In that low moment, the reality of Christ's resurrection became personally redemptive. His writings from that time forward reflected his new conviction.

In verses 12-19, Paul explores some of the personal consequences of denying the resurrection of Christ. He does not say that anyone in Corinth was actually doing that, but he does indicate that some of them were having problems with the idea of dead bodies being brought back to life. For Paul, the denial of the general idea of the resurrection of the dead also meant that one must reject the possibility that Christ was raised. If one rejected Christ's resurrection, the personal consequences were serious.

Paul begins by asking how anyone can deny the reality of the dead being raised if they have accepted the preaching about

Christ's resurrection. Paul has already reminded them that they have accepted and believed this teaching. What amazes him is that some people cannot see the connection between Christ's resurrection and the raising of other people's dead bodies. The fact is, many people today do not see the connection because it is not self-evident. One has to understand some of Paul's presuppositions to see the connection.

First of all, for Paul, the resurrection was an end-time event. He shared the belief of many Jews that God would raise the dead at the end of the age. This view is reflected in the story of Lazarus in John 11. When Jesus told Martha that her brother would rise again, she answered, "I know that he will rise again in the resurrection on the last day" (Jn 11:24). For Paul, the resurrection of Jesus was a signal that the "last day" had begun to unfold. At the appropriate time, the rest of the dead would also be raised. Jesus was the "first fruits" of the harvest, and the rest would be harvested when Jesus returned (v. 23). The resurrection of Jesus, then, was tied to the resurrection of the others.

Secondly, Paul understood the resurrection to involve people's bodies. God did not rescue Jesus' soul from its bodily prison; God raised up Jesus' body and transformed it. Likewise, the bodies of believers will be raised up and transformed. This aspect of resurrection was what proved troubling to some in Corinth. The idea that the body had any enduring worth was alien to their thinking. They could accept the idea of a spiritual afterlife but not a bodily one.

For Paul, to reject the idea of raised bodies is to reject the hope for future life. After all, that life involves a body, although it is a transformed one (vv. 42-44). To reject that future hope is to reject the reality of Christ's bodily resurrection, for his resurrection is tied to the bodily resurrection of others. Paul's argument is built on the basis of these two presuppositions.

Before dealing with his two presuppositions, however, Paul first considers the personal consequences of denying the resurrection of Christ. First of all, it means that his preaching and the Corinthians' acceptance of it have been in vain (v. 14). He has proclaimed and they have believed something that is not true. Secondly, it means that their faith is meaningless and they are still dead in their sins (v. 17). Furthermore, all those who have died believing have simply perished, for there is no afterlife of any kind (v. 18). If there is no afterlife, and Christ only has significance for this life, then all believers are pitiable fools (v. 19).

His last point raises some eyebrows. Would it not be better to live now for Christ, to follow his teachings now, to practice Christian love now, and to try to improve the world in his name— even if there is no afterlife—than not to do so? For Paul, even though such a life might be virtuous, noble, and more commendable than one of immoral self-indulgence, it would still be pitiable. It would be based on an understanding of God that is too limited. It would be rooted in the resignation that the gospel's message of God's ultimate triumph over evil is a pipedream. It would abdicate our hopes for justice to the realities of an unjust world. It would sadly accept that human life has no ultimate value or meaning beyond the few fleeting moments we have here. For some, such a perspective would be considered "realistic." For Paul, it would be pitiable.

Notes

Notes

_____

_____

_____

_____

_____

_____

_____

_____

_____

_____

_____

_____

_____

_____

_____

_____

3

CONTEMPLATE
THE MYSTERY

1 Corinthians 15:20-41

Central Question

What questions or doubts do I have about the resurrection of Christ?

Scripture

1 Corinthians 15:20-41 20 But in fact Christ has been raised from the dead, the first fruits of those who have died. 21 For since death came through a human being, the resurrection of the dead has also come through a human being; 22 for as all die in Adam, so all will be made alive in Christ. 23 But each in his own order: Christ the first fruits, then at his coming those who belong to Christ. 24 Then comes the end, when he hands over the kingdom to God the Father, after he has destroyed every ruler and every authority and power. 25 For he must reign until he has put all his enemies under his feet. 26 The last enemy to be destroyed is death. 27 For "God has put all things in subjection under his feet." But when it says, "All things are put in subjection," it is plain that this does not include the one who put all things in subjection under him. 28 When all things are subjected to him, then the Son himself will also be subjected to the one who put all things in subjection under him, so that God may be all in all. 29 Otherwise, what will those people do who receive baptism on behalf of the dead? If the dead are not raised at all, why are people baptized on their behalf? 30 And why are we putting ourselves in danger every hour? 31 I die every day! That is as certain, brothers and sisters, as my boasting of you—a boast that

I make in Christ Jesus our Lord. 32 If with merely human hopes I fought with wild animals at Ephesus, what would I have gained by it? If the dead are not raised, "Let us eat and drink, for tomorrow we die." 33 Do not be deceived: "Bad company ruins good morals." 34 Come to a sober and right mind, and sin no more; for some people have no knowledge of God. I say this to your shame. 35 But someone will ask, "How are the dead raised? With what kind of body do they come?" 36 Fool! What you sow does not come to life unless it dies. 37 And as for what you sow, you do not sow the body that is to be, but a bare seed, perhaps of wheat or of some other grain. 38 But God gives it a body as he has chosen, and to each kind of seed its own body. 39 Not all flesh is alike, but there is one flesh for human beings, another for animals, another for birds, and another for fish. 40 There are both heavenly bodies and earthly bodies, but the glory of the heavenly is one thing, and that of the earthly is another. 41 There is one glory of the sun, and another glory of the moon, and another glory of the stars; indeed, star differs from star in glory.

Reflecting

Writer and speaker Will Campbell reminisces about a time when neither he nor his wife were working outside the home, and times became rather difficult without the support of a regular paycheck. According to Campbell, one day his wife remarked that one of them had to get a job. Campbell says he sensed his wife had a preference as to which one it should be, so he began his search. Eventually he began to help his friend Willie Nelson organize his concerts.

One day as they traveled on the tour bus, Campbell quietly asked Nelson, "Willie, what do you believe?" Nelson thought for a minute, Campbell remembers, before quietly nodding his head and saying, "Yes." Campbell reflects that often Christians spend too much time arguing over the finer points of theology and too little time learning from each other and cultivating unity in diversity.

In truth, mystery is a part of our faith. If we knew everything—every detail about our God—we would have no need of faith, for faith is believing without seeing.

Studying

Not only were the Corinthian Christians divided about Christian practices such as the observance of the Lord's Supper; they were also divided about matters of theology. As we explored in last week's session, some of the Corinthians did not believe in a future resurrection. Paul stressed the centrality of this belief for Christian faith.

This session's Scripture passage is a continuation of Paul's teaching. If someone had asked Paul what he believed about the resurrection, like Willie Nelson he would have responded with a resounding, "Yes." In the verses we study this week, Paul continues to emphasize the necessity of belief in Christ's resurrection.

How difficult is it for you to affirm something as true when you don't completely understand it?

But Paul goes further. In these verses, Paul affirms his faith in the resurrection, and he also develops a mature theological reflection on its meaning and implications. In verses 20-28 he contrasts Jesus and Adam. Like Adam, Christ stands at the beginning of a new order of things. But while Adam brought death into the world, Christ brought life through his resurrection. He is the "first fruits" of those who have died because his resurrection, like the beginning of the harvest, is a foreshadowing of what lies in store for those who believe in him.

Some of the Christians at Corinth were being baptized in the name of people who had already died. No one is entirely sure what it meant to "receive baptism on behalf of the dead" (v. 29). Mormonism teaches that these individuals were being baptized on behalf of loved ones who had died without becoming Christians. By being baptized, these Christians thought they could secure a place for the dead in the resurrection.

Another possibility is that these Christians were being baptized for those who had not had a chance to be baptized before their deaths. Again, this practice was a way of affirming and assuring that God would raise these departed ones in the resurrection.

Finally, it may be that these Christians were being baptized in memory of the faithful martyrs who had paid the ultimate sacrifice to bring them the gospel message (see vv. 30-31). Therefore, their baptism was meant to commemorate the ministries of preachers and apostles who had gone before.

Whatever the Corinthian believers intended by this practice, there is no evidence that Paul endorsed it. In fact, it is mentioned nowhere else in Scripture. Paul was merely appealing to the Corinthians' familiarity with the practice in order to support his point. If these people did not believe in the resurrection, why were they being baptized in the name of those who had already died? Was it not because they had hope in the resurrection?

After this appeal, Paul continues to develop his resurrection theology. Why, Paul asked, would he be willing to put his life in peril every hour of every day if he did not believe in the resurrection? Paul had been threatened, jailed, run out of town, and almost killed. He had even fought "wild beasts" in Ephesus. Roman law did not allow for Roman citizens like Paul to fight in the arena with wild animals. Paul is likely referring to the many conflicts and trials in which he almost lost his life. Paul had been persecuted as harshly as he had persecuted Christians before his Damascus Road experience. Why would he endure these things if he did not believe? Paul stood behind his faith in the resurrection, even if it might lead to his own death.

> **?** Where do you find strength when your faith comes under attack?

Paul continues that if the resurrection did not take place, it would be reasonable to live without any moral concerns. He urges the Corinthian Christians not to be deceived by people who do not believe in the resurrection and who live with no sense of morality. He seems to be saying, "Why would you be concerned about morality if there were no resurrection?"

Paul ends his appeal with a strong closing argument. Whoever says the resurrection is unnecessary has no knowledge of God. Bluntly, Paul tells the Corinthians, "Some of you really do not know God."

But then Paul continues his exploration of the doctrine of the resurrection. Apparently, the Corinthian Christians were arguing about what kind of bodies they would have at the last resurrection. Paul cautions them not to confuse earthly bodies with spiritual ones. To explain, the Apostle gives an analogy of different kinds of earthly bodies. Each kind of seed produces its own kind of plant. Similarly, people have one kind of body while animals, birds, and fish have other kinds of bodies. In the same way, resurrection bodies will not be like earthly ones because they will be transformed.

> Very truly, I tell you, unless a grain of wheat falls into the earth and dies, it remains just a single grain; but if it dies, it bears much fruit. (Jn 12:24)

At this point, Paul seems to admonish the Corinthians not to be overly concerned with the details of the resurrection. It's interesting to note that Paul did not tell these Christians not to ask questions. He simply cautioned them against becoming so focused on debating the details that they missed the point of believing in the resurrection.

Understanding

According to Paul, there are certain distinctive elements of the Christian faith. A hymn writer expressed his thoughts on distinctive elements of Christianity in this way: "This is the threefold truth on which we take our stand. Christ has died; Christ is risen; Christ will come again" (Green, 408).

Keeping faith confessions broad affirms the mystery of our faith. Sometimes Christians today, not unlike those in ancient Corinth, argue over matters of belief until they become more exclusive than inclusive of those with diverse beliefs.

Admittedly, Paul's words in these verses may be difficult to understand. Perhaps we would do well to remember that at the core of Paul's teaching is an emphasis on the fact of resurrection rather than on the minute details. The resurrection truly is a mystery. Affirming this point helps us find unity in diversity today.

And yet, we need not use this simple confession of faith as a reason to avoid contemplating the mystery. On the contrary, Jesus himself reminded his followers that the greatest commandment is to love the Lord with all our hearts, souls, and minds and to love our neighbors as ourselves (Mk 12:29-31). To love God with all our minds means using our God-given intellects to contemplate and reflect on the meaning of Scripture and Christian beliefs. Resurrection is indeed a mystery, but it is one that we should contemplate and explore.

We must not contemplate the mystery in isolation, however. We learn best when we dialogue about Scripture in the context of community, sharing our thoughts with each other so that we all grow together in our faith. Scripture is dynamic, and no one has the final word concerning its interpretation. Continuing to ponder the wonders and mysteries of Scripture together gives us fresh insights about the resurrection as well as about other distinctive teachings of our faith.

In fact, having doubts or questions about the specifics of the resurrection is not necessarily negative. One of my former pastors regularly reminded the congregation that the Bible moves ahead on its great questions. All the major characters of the Bible had questions, and sometimes God even had questions for them. What do we ask of God today? What might God be asking of us? Voicing our questions and listening for God's voice is part of using our minds to grow closer to our Creator.

What About Me?

• *Christ's resurrection is ultimately a mystery.* Affirming the mystery surrounding this significant element of our faith in no way diminishes the importance of belief in the resurrection. Rather, it opens doors for us to explore the mystery further.

• *The meaning of Christ's resurrection is also a mystery.* Paul linked the resurrection of Christ to the future resurrection of all believers. Affirming this element of faith is also a way for us to cultivate unity in diversity. We may disagree about exactly what happened and why, but we can agree that Jesus died and rose so that we, too, may rise from death one day and live forever with him.

• *Contemplating the mystery of the resurrection is as important as affirming its mystery.* Jesus charged his followers to love God with their minds, not to tune out in the face of mystery. Mystery is something to be considered carefully, not something to be ignored.

• *We should not be afraid of asking questions.* Sometimes questions are the edge of a growing point. Without asking questions, it would be difficult to grow in further understanding of Scripture and beliefs based on Scripture.

References

Raymond B. Brown, "1 Corinthians," *The Broadman Bible Commentary*, vol. 10 (Nashville: Broadman, 1970).

Will Campbell, *Soul Among Lions* (Louisville: Westminster/John Knox, 1999).

Fred Pratt Green, "This Is the Threefold Truth," *The Baptist Hymnal* (Nashville: Convention Press, 1991).

CONTEMPLATE
THE MYSTERY
1 Corinthians 15:20-41

Introduction

Christopher Hitchens one published a book titled *God Is Not
Great*. In the book he does not actually attack God, mainly
because he does not believe in God. Instead, he attacks religion,
which he thinks poisons all of life and threatens meaningful existence and true ethical living. For him, the question of God is a
pointless one. We would do well to shelve all our questions about
God and abandon our attempts to answer them. Of course, that
is not likely to happen for most people.

In a real sense, questions about the resurrection are questions
about God, not questions about us. We may wonder about life
after death. Is it real? What will it be like? When does it happen?
Fundamentally, though, we are asking, What is God up to? If we
believe in God and believe that God is good, we may despair of
the suffering and sorrow that fill this life. How could a good God
let certain things happen? The despair—and the disillusionment
it sometimes brings—may even lead us to doubt that God exists.
If we hold on to our belief in God and God's goodness, the
conviction that there is more than this life allows us to trust that
God will set things right. Many people such as Hitchens think
people believe in God because they want to believe in life after
death. I think it is the other way around. I think we believe in life
after death because we believe in God and we believe that God is
great.

In 1 Corinthians 15:12-19, Paul points out the personal
consequences of denying that Christ rose from the dead. He
immediately turns in verse 20 to affirm the reality of the resurrection and describe how the resurrection of believers will unfold as

part of God's ultimate victory (vv. 20-28). He then asserts that faithful living is futile if there is no resurrection of believers (vv. 29-34). Finally, he begins to describe the nature of resurrection existence (vv. 35-41). That description continues into next week's passage (vv. 42-57).

I. The Resurrection and God's Ultimate Victory (vv. 20-28)

In this section, Paul uses two metaphors to describe what will happen at the end and then interprets each metaphor with references to Scripture. The first metaphor is that of the harvest. Paul likens the resurrected Jesus to the "first fruits" of a harvest. Everything does not ripen at once. Whether peaches or peanuts (common crops here in Georgia), some produce ripens earlier than others. Days or weeks may separate the first fruits from the final harvest. In the case of deceased believers, they may lie in the ground for years or centuries before the resurrection. Yet, the resurrection of Jesus and the resurrection of all believers are part of a single event, according to Paul. To reinforce this idea, Paul alludes to the story of Adam in Genesis. Death came to the human race through one man, Adam. Likewise, resurrection has come through the one man, Jesus. All are united with Adam in death, but in Christ all are united in life. The universalism implied here is qualified by verse 23, where Paul specifies that only those who belong to Christ are raised.

In verse 23, Paul introduces a military metaphor. Here Paul clarifies that not everyone's resurrection happens at the same time. They are raised according to their own "rank" or "corps." The word usually translated order (*tagma*) is a military term denoting divisions of soldiers. Christ, the general, is raised first. Then the troops, believers. The military imagery continues as Paul describes the final campaign. Christ destroys every rule, authority, and power, and then delivers the kingdom to God. The terms "rule, authority, and power" have metaphorical significance like the similar terms in Ephesians 6:12 that refer to spiritual powers. We should not forget, however, where such power was most visibly manifested in Paul's day. The Roman Empire dominated his world. The political implications of his proclamation that God would ultimately subdue all powers would not have been lost on the citizens of the Roman colony of Corinth. Paul affirms that Christ's conquests will ultimately include even the power that holds sway over all mortals: death.

To support his assertion that Christ's victory over the powers will be complete, Paul quotes two psalms. The reference to "putting all his enemies under his feet" comes from Psalm 110:1. The quotation in verse 27, "God has put all things in subjection under his feet," is from Psalm 8:6. Paul interprets both psalms, which in their original contexts referred to a king in Jerusalem (Ps 110) or to humankind in general (Ps 8), as references to Christ and his eventual triumph over all things. Just as Paul clarified that not everyone is resurrected at once, he specifies here that "all things" certainly does not include God. When Christ has subdued everything else, then Christ, the Son, will subject himself to the rule of the one who gave him victory over his enemies. A few centuries after Paul, Arians and others used his words to support a subordinationist view of Christ. Paul was not attempting to lay out a full trinitarian theology here; he was focused on showing that the resurrection of the body was a part of God's plan for creation. Nor was Paul espousing pantheism when he wrote that Christ's victory would lead to God's being "all in all." His point was that ultimately God would prevail over all things.

II. The Resurrection and Faithful Living (vv. 29-34)

In one of my pastorates, I baptized a new convert who had already been baptized more than thirty times. He had been a Mormon, and his baptisms were what that church calls "proxy baptisms." They believe one can be baptized on behalf of dead relatives who were not baptized into the Mormon church during their lives. Guided by this conviction, the Mormon church has built one of the most extensive systems of genealogical records in the world today. They take seriously the responsibility to seek out the names of all relatives and to be baptized on their behalf.

This idea came from a literal reading of 1 Corinthians 15:29: "Otherwise, what will those who are being baptized on behalf of the dead do? If the dead are not raised at all, why are they also baptized for them?" This is a perplexing verse. The most literal way to understand it is that some Corinthian Christians were being baptized vicariously for those who had died unbaptized. On the basis of Paul's views about baptism expressed elsewhere, it is difficult to see him condoning such a practice. The fact that he does not appear to challenge it here has led many interpreters to assume Paul refers to something other than vicarious baptism. Some argue that certain converts were being baptized primarily because they wanted to see their dead loved ones—baptized Christians—again. Another view is that "the dead" refers to "dead bodies." Throughout 1 Corinthians 15, Paul could be using the Greek word for "dead" (*nekros*) to mean corpse since other ancient writers often used the word that way. Some Corinthians had doubts about corpses being raised from the dead. They saw the body as important only for this life. At death, the body would be left behind. "So," Paul asks them, "if the body is not going to be resurrected, then why are people bothering to have their bodies baptized?" This view fits with Paul's emphasis throughout 1 Corinthians on taking what one does with the body seriously. It also fits with his concern for faithful living in the rest of this section.

Paul points to the futility of faithful living if there is no resurrection of the body. "Why are we in danger every hour?" "I die every day," and for what purpose? "What good does it do if I fight the beasts at Ephesus?" These statements do not seem to have any real connection to each other unless we add Paul's quotation of Isaiah 22:13: "Let us eat and drink, for tomorrow we die." If the dead are not raised, then there is no point in struggling now to control the passions of the body. His reference to "fighting beasts" does not mean that he actually tangled with wild animals in the arena in Ephesus (where he happened to be when he wrote this letter). He is using a common metaphor for struggling with the body's passions. What's the use of controlling the body's cravings if this body is going to end up dead and rotting in the ground? We may as well live it up!

Then Paul issues a stern warning by quoting a slogan that also appears in a few ancient writings: "Bad company ruins good morals" (v. 33). The statement appears in a play about prostitutes by Menander. The word for "company" was often used for "banquet companions," many of whom may have been prostitutes. Earlier in the letter Paul warned about indulging in fleshly appetites (6:12-20), and this concern rises again here. Some thought it was fine to pursue such appetites since that is what the body was for and none could enjoy them after death. Paul tells them to "sober up" and sin no more. Their cavalier attitude about the body proves that they were shamefully ignorant about God and God's plans for the body.

III. The Resurrection and Future Existence (vv. 35-41)

In these verses Paul finally speaks directly to the objection that some of the Corinthians apparently had about the idea of bodily resurrection. He puts a pair of questions in the mouth of an imaginary individual who represents their position. This device, known as the diatribe, was often used in ancient arguments. Paul has his imaginary objector ask, "How are the dead raised? With what kind of body do they come?" The second question gets to the heart of the matter. Physical bodies age, die, and decompose. How can they be resuscitated in any kind of meaningful form?

To answer this question, Paul draws once more from his storage of agricultural metaphors. But first, he ridicules the erroneous assumption behind the stated question by calling his imaginary interrogator a "fool." "Do you not understand how planting works? When you plant seed, the seed has to die before it grows something." His statement calls to mind Jesus' words in John 12:24: "Unless a grain of wheat falls into the earth and dies, it remains alone; but if it dies, it bears much fruit." In fact, the planted seed does not "die," but it does cease to be a seed. It becomes transformed into something far more significant than what it was. As Jesus' parable about the seed growing secretly (Mk 4:26-29) points out, the transformation of a seed into something else is a mystery. The sower does not know how it happens. The transformation is mysterious because it is God's doing, not ours. God gives the seed the body God chooses. As it is with plants, so it is with animals, Paul points out. God gives different bodies to fish, birds, other animals, and human beings. The same is true for heavenly "bodies." These celestial bodies are different from earthly bodies, and each has its own "glory," or "uniqueness."

Among the heavenly bodies, the sun, moon, and stars have different defining characteristics. Even the different stars have their own unique modes of existence.

Paul's discussion of bodies of various kinds makes two main points. First, existence involves embodiment. Other than God, everything that has life is embodied in some form. Even the sun, moon, and stars (which most people in antiquity viewed as living things because they move across the sky) have bodies. So it is with the life beyond. For Paul, that form of existence also involved a body of some kind. Secondly, there is both continuity and discontinuity between the body of this life and the body of the next. This earthly body of flesh does die, but it does not pass away into nothingness. It is transformed into the resurrection body. That resurrection body is different in form from the pre-resurrection body, but it is the same body. Exactly what form it will have is Paul's focus in the next section (15:42-49).

Notes

Notes

4

REJOICE
IN HOPE

1 Corinthians 15:42-58

Central Question

What hope for the future do I find in the resurrection of Christ?

Scripture

1 Corinthians 15:42-58 42 So it is with the resurrection of the dead. What is sown is perishable, what is raised is imperishable. 43 It is sown in dishonor, it is raised in glory. It is sown in weakness, it is raised in power. 44 It is sown a physical body, it is raised a spiritual body. If there is a physical body, there is also a spiritual body. 45 Thus it is written, "The first man, Adam, became a living being"; the last Adam became a life-giving spirit. 46 But it is not the spiritual that is first, but the physical, and then the spiritual. 47 The first man was from the earth, a man of dust; the second man is from heaven. 48 As was the man of dust, so are those who are of the dust; and as is the man of heaven, so are those who are of heaven. 49 Just as we have borne the image of the man of dust, we will also bear the image of the man of heaven. 50 What I am saying, brothers and sisters, is this: flesh and blood cannot inherit the kingdom of God, nor does the perishable inherit the imperishable. 51 Listen, I will tell you a mystery! We will not all die, but we will all be changed, 52 in a moment, in the twinkling of an eye, at the last trumpet. For the trumpet will sound, and the dead will be raised imperishable, and we will be changed. 53 For this perishable body must put on imperishability, and this mortal body must put on immortality. 54 When this perishable body puts on imperishability, and this mortal body puts on immortality, then the saying that is written will be fulfilled: "Death has been swallowed up in victory." 55 "Where, O death, is your victory? Where, O death, is your sting?" 56 The sting of death is sin, and the power of sin is the law. 57 But thanks be to God, who gives us the victory through our Lord Jesus Christ. 58 Therefore, my beloved, be steadfast, immovable, always excelling in the work of the Lord, because you know that in the Lord your labor is not in vain.

Reflecting

In *Dakota: A Spiritual Geography*, writer Kathleen Norris describes a vast prairie and farmland many people would consider desolate. Focusing on the sparsely populated rural area in which she is a minister, she describes how she could drive for miles without seeing a sign giving directions to any town. In particular, she describes the lonely roads she traveled on the unmarked way to a town called Hope. Eventually, she arrived there, but the trip was long and trying.

I know how she felt. More than twenty years ago when I lived in Arkansas, my parents moved to another town in Louisiana. Everyone who knows me well knows my sense of direction is less than good. If I come to a familiar intersection from a different direction, for just a moment I have absolutely no idea where I am. I have learned to compensate by looking for signs that point me in the right direction, but if signs aren't there, I'm lost. If I think I need to turn left, there's a good chance that I need to turn right! So when my parents moved to this new town, I had a challenge. The best way to get there from where I lived was go to through a town called Hope, Arkansas.

My first trip to my parents' house went well until I got to the country roads of western Arkansas. I seemed to be driving further than I intended. I found myself looking for a sign directing me to Hope.

Later in her book of reflections, Kathleen Norris describes a spirituality that comes from the Dakota people's connection with the land. For instance, in one early November scene, she portrays mourners who kneel beside the open ground at a graveside funeral service. They were farmers and ranchers, she explains, who were checking the earth for moisture, looking for a sign of hope.

What "signs of hope" do you see today in your spiritual life? In your family? In your church?

We all search for hope at some point. Perhaps our search comes after the loss of a job. Maybe it comes after the unexpected or even expected death of a loved one. Perhaps it comes when a relationship is broken. Or perhaps our search for hope comes when we feel so overwhelmed by life that we don't know which way to turn. For whatever reason, we all need to find hope at some time in our lives.

This session's Scripture passage offers us hope in the resurrection. There comes a time, Paul says, when all perishable life will be imperishable. Our labor in this life will not be in vain.

Studying

Continuing where we ended last week's session, Paul's discussion in today's passage concerns the nature of resurrected bodies. Paul sets up analogies to distinguish between the body that dies and the body that is resurrected from the dead.

First, Paul says what is sown is perishable, but what is raised is imperishable. In other words, the body that dies is perishable but the resurrected body is imperishable. The earthly body is subject to decay because it is part of a world that is subject to corruption. But the resurrected body is free from corruption.

Second, the buried body is characterized by dishonor, while the resurrection body is marked by glory or splendor. Likewise, the body that dies is characterized by physical and spiritual weakness, but the resurrected body is strong and powerful.

Finally, the body that dies is a limited physical body, but the resurrected body is a spiritual body energized by the Spirit of God, fit for life with God who is Spirit.

The resurrection of believers is a transformation from one kind of existence to another, but it does not entirely erase the physical aspects of the former life. As Richard Wilson observes,

> The antitheses developed in 1 Cor 15:42-50 lay equal stress on the continuity and the discontinuity between the "physical body" and "spiritual body." Paul contends that something of the image of the physical endures through the resurrection transformation although he emphatically states "flesh and blood cannot inherit the kingdom of God" (1 Cor 15:50). Significantly, the same point is implied through the evangelists' descriptions of resurrection appearances. The risen one is the crucified one, yet somehow different (Matt 28:9ff.; Luke 24:13:ff; John 20–21). (755)

Paul then compares the physical body to the body of Adam and the spiritual body to the body of Christ. Adam was earthly, formed from the dust of the earth (Gen 2:7). Adam became a living, physical being. Likewise, all humanity is made from dust, bearing the image of Adam. Paul does not describe the physical body as bad, however; only as perishable. Like most Jews, Paul understood human beings, both body and soul, to be part of God's good creation (see Gen 1:31). There is no dualistic emphasis on the body as evil or unworthy of redemption, although merely physical existence must be transcended. Our earliest ancestor was a living though mortal being on earth. In contrast, Christ, "the last Adam" (15:45) and "the second man" (15:47), came from heaven so that human beings could ultimately bear his image.

Paul continues by describing the mystery of the resurrection once again. The focus is not on death but on the change that will happen "in the twinkling of an eye" (15:52) at the resurrection.

Mortal bodies will become immortal, and death will be swallowed up in victory.

Paul ends with words reminiscent of the prophets: "Where, O death, is your victory? Where, O death, is your sting?" The prophet Isaiah affirmed that God would swallow up death forever, and the Lord would wipe away the tears from all eyes (Isa 25:8). Similarly, the prophet Hosea asks, "O Death, where are your plagues? O Sheol, where is your destruction?" (Hos 13:14).

Paul brings his discussion of the resurrection to a close by thanking God who gives us this victory over death through Jesus Christ (15:57). Since he has this hope, he can conclude his message with words of encouragement: "Therefore, my beloved, be steadfast, immovable, always excelling in the work of the Lord, because you know that in the Lord your labor is not in vain" (15:58). Paul encourages the Corinthian Christians to keep working for the glory of God because, in the end, their hard work will bring victory.

Understanding

Paul's words are just as encouraging for us today as they were for the Corinthian Christians. Often, these final words of Paul are read as a comfort at funerals of Christians. We who have lost loved ones still grieve deeply, yet we do not grieve as those who have no hope.

But Paul's words are also encouraging to those of us who may be struggling with our faith journey. Life brings difficulties, and Christians are certainly not immune to them. Like everyone else, Christians lose employment, experience broken relationships, suffer illnesses, encounter injustice, and lose loved ones to death.

Sometimes, in the midst of our deepest struggles, Christians understandably become discouraged. The mystic John of the Cross called these deepest struggles the dark night of the soul. We usually emerge from these times as stronger people, but while we endure them, we feel weak. These words of Paul remind us that we do not struggle in vain. The final victory will be ours in Christ.

The spirituals written and sung by slaves reflected this hope in future victory. No matter how much they suffered on earth—and their suffering was immeasurable—they placed their hope in the life to come. Songs such as "Swing Low, Sweet Chariot," "Steal Away to Jesus," and "Wade in the Water" were a theology of hope expressed in song.

Some of our familiar old hymns offer similar words of hope. When we sing "We'll Work 'til Jesus Comes," "Shall We Gather at the River," and "Victory in Jesus," we voice our hope in the life to come.

Hope in the life to come, of course, does not take the place of justice here on earth. But when we encounter life's struggles, it is encouraging to know that not even death will be able to overcome the victory we have through the resurrection of Christ.

> **Hope**
>
> The sins against hope are despair, as anticipated failure, and presumption, as anticipated fulfillment. In both these cases man seeks to break out of his pilgrim existence and have his life otherwise than from the hand of God.
> —Ferdinand Kerstiens
>
> Hope is hearing the melody of the future. Faith is to dance to it now.
> —Ruben Alves
>
> Hope means expectancy when things are otherwise hopeless.
> —G. K. Chesterton
>
> Hope is the best possession. None are completely wretched but those who are without hope, and few are reduced so low as that.
> —William Hazlitt
>
> The future is as bright as the promises of God.
> —Adoniram Judson

What About Me?

• *We have hope that death is not the end.* When we are grieving the loss of a loved one, we can find comfort in Paul's words to the Corinthians. Ultimately, Christ has the victory over even death.

• *We have hope that what we do as Christ followers truly matters.* When we are grieving losses of other kinds—a lost job, loss of children, loss of a relationship—we can also find comfort in Paul's words that our work here on earth is not done in vain.

• *We have hope that God is ever present with us, even during trials.* In the midst of our struggles, we can still find an example to follow in Paul's words, thanking God for seeing us through the struggles.

Resources

Raymond Brown, "I Corinthians," *The Broadman Bible Commentary*, vol. 10 (Nashville: Broadman, 1970).

Kathleen Norris, *Dakota: A Spiritual Geography* (New York: Houghton Mifflin, 1993).

Richard F. Wilson, "Resurrection in the New Testament," *Mercer Dictionary of the Bible*, ed. Watson E. Mills et al. (Macon GA: Mercer University Press, 1990).

REJOICE
IN HOPE

1 Corinthians 15:42-58

Introduction

Clarence Jordan was a New Testament scholar and translator whose "Cotton Patch" version of the Gospels inspired a musical by the same name. He is better remembered, though, as a prophetic voice and activist on behalf of civil rights. His vision of racial unity led him to establish an integrated Christian community in Georgia, Koinonia Farm. It also earned him the wrath and hostility of many in the white community in South Georgia, including most Baptist churches there. When he died, he was buried at Koinonia in a plain cedar box. Millard Fuller, a resident of the farm and the founder of Habitat for Humanity, delivered the eulogy. After Jordan was buried, Fuller's two-year-old daughter spontaneously broke into a simple song:

> Happy birthday to you.
> Happy birthday to you.
> Happy birthday, dear Clarence.
> Happy birthday to you.

To see death as an occasion for rejoicing may strike some as inappropriate or insensitive to the grief of the survivors. The sting of death is real, and any flippant remark to the effect that the deceased has "gone to a better place" overlooks the pain that death inflicts upon us. Nonetheless, in the midst of our real and appropriate grief, the hope embedded in a child's simple song can give us cause to trust that death does not have the final word. Those who die "in the Lord" have a reason to look forward to that coming day of new birth.

Having made his case for the importance of believing in the resurrection of the body, Paul now describes the nature of the resurrected body and the mysterious transformation that will take place. This, he holds, is the sure ground for trusting that what we do for the Lord in our present bodies is not in vain.

I. The Glory of the Resurrection Body (vv. 42-49)

In the previous section, Paul pointed out that the resurrected body is different from the earthly body. Now he elaborates on that difference. The earthly body is perishable, lowly, weak, made of dust, and bearing the image of the first man, Adam. The resurrected body is imperishable, glorious, powerful, heavenly, and bearing the image of Christ. Paul's emphasis here is on the difference between the two. Elsewhere in this letter, he highlights the significance of the earthly body, so we misconstrue the point of his contrasts if we think he depicts earthly existence as wretched. In comparison to the resurrection body, our present bodies are clearly inferior, but that does not mean they are worthless.

Paul's label for the earthly body is difficult to translate into English. He calls it a *soma psychikon*, which literally means something like "soulful body." To translate it as "physical body" obscures the distinction he wants to make, since the resurrected body is also in some sense "physical," though in a different way. Paul does not pose body over against soul, nor does he pose body over against spirit. He juxtaposes soul and spirit. The "soulful body" is a body invigorated by the vital force of life that the Bible often refers to as the soul. Paul recalls the account in Genesis where God breathed into Adam the breath of life and he became a "living soul" (v. 45). Like Adam, we are living souls embodied in a frail form made from the elements of the earth. The soul and the body are one, not two separate entities that can be disentangled. When the life force desists, the body dies and perishes. Conversely, when the body dies, the life force desists; it does not go marching on.

The difficulty of explaining this clearly is evident in Paul's use of "spiritual body" (*soma pneumatikon*). If we think of the body as primarily material, then Paul's reference to "spiritual matter" appears to be an oxymoron. For Paul, the body is who and what we are. It is our physical self, but it is also our emotional and mental self. It is all that we are except for the life force, the soul, which God has breathed into us. This body, as we now experience it, cannot experience the new life ahead. That life calls for a transformation of this body into the glorious state of the resurrection body. The gospel song that claims "I'll have a new body" is partly correct, but it gives the impression that this old body will be left behind. Paul's conviction is not that this old body will be replaced but rather that it will be transformed. The resurrection body will not be invigorated by the time-bound soul but by the eternal spirit.

The soulful body bears the image of Adam (v. 49). That is, we as human beings possess those qualities that Adam as the archetypal human being possessed, both good and bad. We possess the ability, with God's help, to care for God's creation and to produce and care for other human beings. We also possess the ability to damage God's creation and harm our fellow human beings. The first Adam received life and these qualities from God, but the second Adam, Christ, gives life and the qualities of resurrection existence (v. 45). The latter half of verse 49 is difficult to translate. Most modern versions read, "*we will* also bear the image of the man of heaven." This fits with Paul's contrast between our bodies now and our resurrected bodies. But nearly all the ancient manuscripts actually read, "*let us* bear the image of the man of heaven." This does not fit well with Paul's main point, but if it is the correct reading, then perhaps Paul was saying that though we have borne the image of Adam, we should now look to Christ and strive to conform our lives to his. Though we do not yet possess the resurrected body that will fully reflect the image of Christ, we should live in such a way that Christ is reflected even in our earthly bodies. Either way, becoming like him is the glory of the resurrection. The full experience of that glory must await our own resurrection, but to the degree that we can reflect the image of Christ now, we can already bear the marks of resurrection existence.

II. The Mystery of Transformation (vv. 50-57)

Thus far, Paul has focused on the resurrection of the dead. But what about the living? Though Paul and others of his day may have expected the resurrection to happen soon, it was still an event in the future for which they had to wait. What if one were able to wait until it actually occurred? What if the early believers' expectation that Christ would come soon had been on target and they found themselves still alive and unburied when it happened? What if those people today who avidly anticipate the Second Coming "any day now" should turn out to be right? What would happen to those who are still alive? Of course, the advocates of "Left Behind" theology think they know exactly what would happen. The living would be "raptured" to meet Jesus in the air. But for them, that does not happen at the resurrection; it happens at some kind of pseudo-return by Christ. According to their pretribulation rapture scenario, the resurrection of the dead happens later, when Christ *really* returns.

While the pretribulationists derive most of their unbiblical and inherently un-Christian view from distortions of Scripture, Paul does have something to say about the fate of the undead at Christ's return. He begins by pointing out that mere mortals of flesh and blood who are still existing only in perishable bodies cannot inherit the kingdom of God. But then, he goes on to divulge a mystery. Not everyone will have to die, but everyone will have to be transformed—the living as well as the dead. Earlier, Paul depicted the victory of God using military imagery, and here, once again, he likens the resurrection to the trumpeter's call to arms. This time, though, it is the last trumpet call, the one signaling victory. In that brief moment, faster than one can blink, the dead will be raised *and* the living will be transformed. Paul reiterates that it is necessary for the perishable, mortal bodies to "put on" imperishability and immortality. By using the language of clothing here, Paul again underscores that there is continuity between this body and the resurrection body. The perishable does not perish; it becomes imperishable.

When all this happens, Paul says, certain Scriptures will have been fulfilled. He quotes Isaiah 25:8: "Death has been swallowed up in victory." The Hebrew text he appears to draw on here actually reads, "He will swallow up death forever." Paul changes the future tense of the verb to a past tense because he is looking at the event from the perspective of the time when it has been fulfilled. What appears in Isaiah 25:8 as a promise becomes a reality in the resurrection. Death, long the great consumer of life, will itself be consumed.

Paul then uses words from Hosea to express a taunting rebuke of death: "Where, O Death, is your victory? Where, O Death, is your sting?" Paul apparently switches to the Greek text of Hosea 13:14 as the source of his quotation because in Hebrew the two statements about death actually express God's judgment on Israel. In the Greek version, though, they are part of God's promise to deliver God's people. The Greek text of Hosea 13:14 also has "penalty" where Paul has "victory." He seems to have altered the wording slightly to emphasize the contrast between God's ultimate victory over death in the quotation from Isaiah and death's final failure to achieve the victory it has always previously known.

Paul adds some commentary to his quotation of Hosea as he continues the contrast between death's usual victory and God's final triumph. He defines the "sting" of death as sin. As in Romans, Paul closely connects sin and death. Sin is the tool death uses to work its way into human life. Death stings human beings again and again through sin until the poison of sin causes one to succumb to death. For Paul, though the law is holy and good, it participates in death's destruction of human life because it identifies sin and, in doing so, makes sin more powerful. Thus, the law is sin's power. But despite the perpetual onslaught of suffering that this trio of terror has inflicted on the human race, the victory over all three destructive powers has been won by God through our Lord Jesus Christ (15:57). The captives have been set free, thanks to God.

III. The Glorious Mystery of Our Present Work (v. 58)

Many of the hymns sung in the church where I grew up were about heaven. "There Is a Land that Is Fairer than Day," "When We All Get to Heaven," and "When the Morning Comes" were frequent requests on "Pick-a-Hymn" night. They are great hymns.

They do, however, reflect a longing for the next life that can sometimes become so obsessive that we do not give enough attention to the here and now. Paul did not share that obsession. No one can doubt that Paul looked forward to God's final triumph and the resurrection of the dead. No one who reads his letters, though, could ever accuse him of neglecting the importance of this life. In fact, in 1 Corinthians, most of what he writes about concerns everyday matters. Only in chapter 15 does he focus on the life to come. If we read the whole letter and look at this chapter in context, we will see that Paul talked about the resurrection *because* some of the Corinthian Christians were not taking this present life seriously enough. They believed that what they did with their earthly bodies was of no eternal consequence. Paul confronted that erroneous perspective by showing the connection between the earthly body and the heavenly one.

We should not be surprised, then, that Paul ends his exploration of resurrection by calling his readers back to the present: "Therefore, my beloved, be steadfast, immovable, always excelling in the work of the Lord, because you know that in the Lord your labor is not in vain" (v. 58). The hope of the resurrection is not an excuse to ignore the demands of this life. Rather, it is the inspiration we need to give this life the attention it requires. It tells us that we do not labor in vain to be the people God wants us to be. What we do now matters. It matters now. It matters for eternity.

Notes

Notes

nextsunday
STUDIES

1 Peter
Keep Hope Alive

This study of First Peter focuses on keeping hope alive in the face of pressures and circumstances that could possibly extinguish it completely, or worse, turn authentic faith into a pale replica of the real thing.

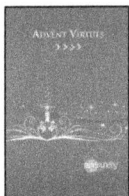

Advent Virtues

The phrase "holiday rush" is not an exaggeration. The frantic pace required to purchase gifts, bake holiday foods, and attend Christmas parties, plays, and performances takes its toll; we arrive at Christmas Day exhausted. Within the context of December busyness, the ancient Christian season of Advent takes on new meaning and acquires renewed importance. May God instill the virtues of *hope, peace, joy, love,* and *faith* in each of us this Advent.

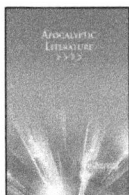

Apocalyptic Literature

This study examines five apocalyptic texts in the Bible—from Zechariah, Daniel, Matthew, and Revelation. With each new year bringing a new prediction of impending doom, it is always a perfect time to get the story straight. Apocalyptic literature does not address the future. It addresses our present.

Approaching a Missional Mindset

The World isn't the same as it once was. We must be the church in a new place, in unimagined ways, and with a wider range of people. Engage your small group with the radical and refreshing challenge of developing a "missional lifestyle."

Baptist Freedom
Celebrating Our Baptist Heritage

What makes a Baptist a Baptist? Of course, the ultimate answer is simple: membership in a local Baptist church. But there are all kinds of Baptist churches! What are the spiritual and theological marks of a Baptist? What is the shape and the feel of Baptist Christianity?

The Bible and the Arts

God has used artistic expression throughout the centuries to convey truth, offer blessing, and urge believers to deeper faithfulness. In modern life, artistic expression flourishes, from movies to books to music to paintings to photographs. Sometimes artists are intentional about trying to portray God's truths. Other times, perhaps God is working even when the artist is unaware of it. As believers, we may hear and see God at work in many art forms.

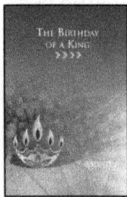

The Birthday of a King

The first four lessons in this unit draw inspiration from a traditional interpretation of the Advent candles as the Prophets' Candle, the Bethlehem Candle, the Shepherds' Candle, and the Angels' Candle. The final lesson, which occurs after Advent, celebrates the theological meaning of Jesus' birth as described in the prologue to John's Gospel.

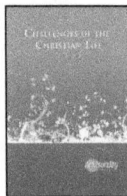

Challenges of the Christian Life

The way of the cross is difficult, and taking Jesus seriously means looking honestly at how we fall short of God's best hopes for us and seeing how much we need God's grace. For all of us there are times when we need to remember that Christ is our saving grace and recommit ourselves to the journey of faith, rediscovering, again and again, the life-giving purpose described in the book of Ephesians.

Christ Is Born!

Even in the midst of difficult circumstances, Advent is a time when we can find hope. Much like today, people in the 1st century church faced struggles. Examining the Gospel of Matthew, lessons include "Waiting for Christ," "Preparing for Christ," "Expecting Christ," "Announcing Christ," and "The Arrival of Christ."

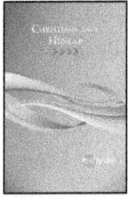

Christians and Hunger

These sessions challenge us to apply gospel lenses and holy imagination to what literally gives us energy to live: food. With God's grace, we have the opportunity to imagine communities where tables are large and all are fed.

Christians and the Public Square

Politics and faith are tricky areas for Christians to negotiate. The First Amendment to the Constitution guarantees religious freedom for all Americans. As Christians who are also citizens, questions abound: How do we distinguish between faithful and unfaithful forms of civic engagement? How do we give Caesar his due while giving our all to God?

Christmas in Mark

In the early chapters of Mark, we will encounter a Christmas story. This story, however, will not be quite like the one told by other Gospel writers, but it will resonate with the reality of your life. Mark doesn't deny the beauty or reality of the nativity; however, he seems to believe that Christmas begins—the gospel begins—when Christ intrudes upon the hard realities of life.

The Church on a Mission

What does it mean to be a church on a mission? The lesson of Acts 1:8 is that we must simultaneously carry out Christ's mandate at home, in our region, in places that have been our blind spots, and around the world.

Colossians
Living the Faith Faithfully

Paul's letter to the Colossians begins with a high-minded philosophical defense of the faith, but concludes with a collection of extremely practical advice for living by faith. This study addresses the questions many Christians face today, helping them apply Paul's practical advice in their own lives.

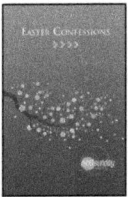

Easter Confessions

Easter confession is often found on many different lips in the Gospel of John. When we listen carefully, those ancient confessions still echo into this new millennium.

Embracing the Word of God

We live during a time of transition in Christian history. Basic assumptions about the truth of the Christian faith are being questioned, not only by nonbelievers, but by Christians themselves. First John offers a starting point for understanding of what it means to "be" Christian.

Esther: A Woman of Discretion and Valor

The book of Esther is not a record of historical facts as such. Rather, it is a magnificent narrative that refuses to interpret life as being driven by coincidence or happenstance. In the otherwise unknown characters of Esther, Haman, and Mordecai, we trace the movement of the divine hand as God collaborates with God's risk-taking people to rescue them from the hand of their enemies.

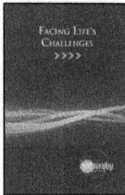

Facing Life's Challenges

This study explores four significant challenges common to most persons of faith: the challenge of new light, the challenge of time's limit, the challenge of living with mystery, and the challenge of authentic spirituality. Although these issues are neither simple nor easy to ponder, this study effectively leads us in confronting these challenges.

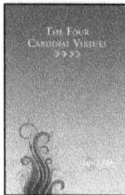

The Four Cardinal Virtues

Christians are learning how to distinguish between members of a church and disciples of Christ. Discipleship involves developing virtues in those who come to our churches seeking life, salvation, grace, mercy. If we want to have something to offer a world in desperate need, then we must return to virtues like discernment, justice, courage, and moderation. We must return to the hard and glorious work of making disciples.

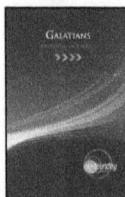

Galatians
Freedom in Christ

Paul wrote with fiery passion, as you will notice from the opening paragraphs of this letter to the Galatians. But his language reveals that he was writing about a crucially important issue—the very nature of salvation in Christ.

A Holy and Surprising Birth

Christmas begins here—discover these five love stories from the book of Luke and renew your appreciation of God's laborious effort to birth our salvation.

How Does the Church Decide?

An array of decisions draw energy and time from church members. These decisions may be theological, such as mode of baptism, aesthetic, such as the color of the sanctuary carpet, or functional, such as the selection of a new minister. This study will consider how the church has made its decisions in the past to help guide our decisions today.

Is God Calling?

Witness the varying forms of God's call, the variety of people called, and the variety of responses. Perhaps God's call to you will become clearer.

James
Gaining True Wisdom

If we'll be honest with God and ourselves as we study what James says, we can make great strides toward wisdom and a living faith.

Life Lessons from Bathsheba

Who was Bathsheba? She was a complex figure who developed from the silent object of David's lust into a powerful, vocal, and influential queen mother.

Life Lessons from David

In the Bible, we catch David in the various stages of the human journey: childhood, adolescence, adulthood, and senior adulthood. From the biblical treatment of the stages of David's life, we can land some insights to assist us in better understanding the human journey.

The Matriarchs

The matriarchs of Genesis offer their lives as a testimony of faith, perseverance, and audacity. We learn from their mistakes and suffering. We will gain the hope of Hagar, the joy of Sarah, and the audacity of Rebekah as we are challenged to examine our prejudices and our insecurities while studying Esau and Jacob's wives.

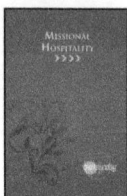

Missional Hospitality

If we are serious about following Jesus, we will be people of open hearts, open hands, and open homes. In other words, as followers of Jesus we will practice the fine art of hospitality. In lesson one, we reflect on hospitality to strangers. In lesson two, we address hospitality to the poor. In lesson three, we focus on hospitality to sinners. In lesson four, we learn about hospitality to newcomers. Lesson five reminds us about our hospitality to Christ.

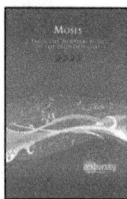

Moses
From the Burning Bush to the Promised Land

We would do well to trace the life of Moses so we might discover how his life changed, both personally and as Israel's leader, as he learned what it meant to love God with all his heart, soul, and strength.

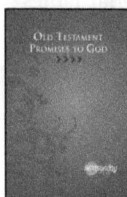

Old Testament Promises to God

Some individuals may feel that our promises couldn't possibly mean anything to God. Perhaps the real question is this: under what circumstances should or do we make such promises? The Old Testament contains several examples of people making promises to God, using the unique form of a biblical "vow."

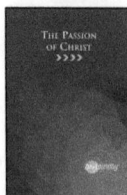

The Passion of Christ

The four lessons in this unit highlight the faith struggles of the early disciples. In lesson one, Jesus addresses the issues of faith and practice. In lesson two, we meet Judas who, like us, struggled with God's Kingdom and human kingdoms. In lesson three, the issue of temptation reminds us that our faith journey is a constant challenge. Lesson Four invites us to remember Peter's experience of "faith failure." Peter's failure, however, is not the final word. There is forgiveness.

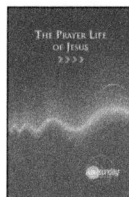

The Prayer Life of Jesus

The study of Jesus' prayer life can deepen our own prayer practices. These five sessions examine the importance of prayer at various stages of Jesus' life and ministry. He made no important decisions without consulting God.

Proverbs for Living

Long ago, a collection of wise teachers committed themselves to the ways of God and collected this wisdom into what we know as the book of Proverbs. These four lessons explore the simple truth of Proverbs: there is a good life to be had—a life lived in faithfulness to God.

Qualities of Our Missional God

Too often we are tempted to let "numbers" drive missions. The book of Numbers reminds us that missions is motivated by something deeper. Missions reflects the heart and nature of God. If we can just get past the math, we can see God's nature clearly in the book of Numbers. . . in the wilderness.

The Seven Deadly Sins

What exactly is sin? Just as we organize our cupboards and our schedules to make sense of our lives, Christian thinkers have organized sin into a number of categories in order to understand and surrender these patterns to God. The notion of "seven deadly sins" emerged as a way to recognize specific dangers to our spiritual lives. The purpose of the book is to guide people away from sin and into a wise and godly life.

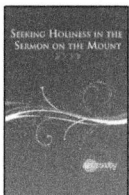

Seeking Holiness in the Sermon on the Mount

The Sermon on the Mount has long been recognized as the pinnacle of Jesus' teaching. But with this importance in mind, it's easy to think of Jesus' teachings as lofty and idealistic, offering little guidance for everyday life. Perhaps Jesus' sermon allows us to see beyond ourselves, beyond our own failures and shortcomings— revealing God's intention for our lives.

Spiritual Disciplines
Obligation or Opportunity?

The spiritual disciplines help deepen a believer's faith and increases his or her intimacy with Christ. In this study, we take a deeper look at some of the disciplines and consider their practice as a response to God's love.

Stewardship
A Way of Living

Great News! Stewardship is not about money! At least not *just* about money. Certainly, stewardship relates to money, and, yes, we need to tithe. However, stewardship branches out into multiple areas of life. Properly practiced, this act of service can lead to peace and purpose in living.

The Ten Commandments

When the Ten Commandments are in the news, it is usually because a judge or teacher has hung them up on the walls. The Ten Commandments do not need to be posted or even preached nearly so much as they need to be practiced and viewed as life-giving, joyful affirmations of a better way of life.

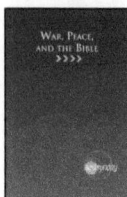

War, Peace, and the Bible

As people of faith, we are faced daily with an expectation that we participate in violent actions, our willingness to allow violence in the world to continue, and our response to violence in our lives. Is there a place for war and violence in our faith?

What Would Jesus Say?
A Lenten Study

To address what Jesus would say, we need to discover what Jesus did say. These lessons will attempt to help us understand Jesus' teachings and apply them today.

NextSunday Studies are available from NextSunday Resources

www.ingramcontent.com/pod-product-compliance
Lightning Source LLC
Chambersburg PA
CBHW060656030426
42337CB00017B/2643